Equipped to Se

Volunteer
Youth Worker
Training
Course

LEADER'S GUIDE

YOUTH SPECIALTIES TITLES

Professional Resources
The Church and the American Teenager (previously released as Growing Up in America)
Developing Spiritual Growth in Junior High Students
Feeding Your Forgotten Soul
Help! I'm a Sunday School Teacher!
Help! I'm a Volunteer Youth Worker!
High School Ministry
How to Recruit and Train Volunteer Youth Workers (previously released as Unsung Heroes)
Junior High Ministry (Revised Edition)
The Ministry of Nurture
Organizing Your Youth Ministry
Peer Counseling in Youth Groups
Advanced Peer Counseling in Youth Groups
The Youth Minister's Survival Guide
Youth Ministry Nuts and Bolts

Discussion Starter Resources
Amazing Tension Getters
Get 'Em Talking
High School TalkSheets
Junior High TalkSheets
High School TalkSheets: Psalms and Proverbs
Junior High TalkSheets: Psalms and Proverbs
More High School TalkSheets
More Junior High TalkSheets
Option Plays
Parent Ministry TalkSheets
Tension Getters
Tension Getters Two

Ideas Library
Ideas Combo 1-4, 5-8, 9-12, 13-16, 17-20, 21-24, 25-28, 29-32, 33-36, 37-40, 41-44, 45-48, 49-52, 53, 54
Ideas Index

Youth Ministry Programming
Adventure Games
Creative Bible Lessons
Creative Programming Ideas for Junior High Ministry
Creative Socials and Special Events
Equipped to Serve
Facing Your Future
Good Clean Fun
Good Clean Fun, Volume 2
Great Fundraising Ideas for Youth Groups
Great Games for City Kids
Great Ideas for Small Youth Groups
Great Retreats for Youth Groups
Greatest Skits on Earth
Greatest Skits on Earth, Volume 2
Holiday Ideas for Youth Groups (Revised Edition)
Hot Illustrations for Youth Talks
Hot Talks
Junior High Game Nights
More Junior High Game Nights
On-Site: 40 On-Location Youth Programs
Play It! Great Games for Groups

Play It Again! More Great Games for Groups
Road Trip
Super Sketches for Youth Ministry
Teaching the Bible Creatively
Teaching the Truth about Sex
Up Close and Personal: How to Build Community in Your Youth Group

4th-6th Grade Ministry
Attention Grabbers for 4th-6th Graders
4th-6th Grade TalkSheets
Great Games for 4th-6th Graders
How to Survive Middle School
Incredible Stories
More Attention Grabbers for 4th-6th Graders
More Great Games for 4th-6th Graders
Quick and Easy Activities for 4th-6th Graders
More Quick and Easy Activities for 4th-6th Graders
Teach 'Toons

Clip Art
ArtSource Volume 1—Fantastic Activities
ArtSource Volume 2—Borders, Symbols, Holidays, and Attention Getters
ArtSource Volume 3—Sports
ArtSource Volume 4—Phrases and Verses
ArtSource Volume 5—Amazing Oddities and Appalling Images
ArtSource Volume 6—Spiritual Topics
Youth Specialties Clip Art Book
Youth Specialties Clip Art Book, Volume 2

Video
Edge TV
God Views
The Heart of Youth Ministry: A Morning with Mike Yaconelli
Next Time I Fall in Love Video Curriculum
Promo Spots for Junior High Game Nights
Resource Seminar Video Series
Understanding Your Teenage Video Curriculum
Witnesses

Student Books
Going the Distance
Good Advice
Grow for It Journal
Grow for It Journal: Through the Scriptures
How to Live with Your Parents without Losing Your Mind
I Don't Remember Dropping the Skunk, But I Do Remember Trying to Breathe
Next Time I Fall in Love
Next Time I Fall in Love Journal
101 Things to Do During a Dull Sermon

Equipped to Serve

Volunteer Youth Worker Training Course

Dennis "Tiger" McLuen

LEADER'S GUIDE

Youth Specialties

ZondervanPublishingHouse
Grand Rapids, Michigan

A Division of HarperCollins Publishers

Youth Specialties Books, 1224 Greenfield Drive, El Cajon, California 92021, are published by Zondervan Publishing House, 5300 Patterson, S.E., Grand Rapids, Michigan 49530.

Edited by Noel Becchetti and Lorraine Triggs
Typography and design by Patton Brothers Design
Cover illustration by Court Patton

Printed in the United States of America

98 99 / MAL / 6 5 4

TABLE OF CONTENTS

ACKNOWLEDGEMENTS 6
INTRODUCTION 7

SECTION ONE: Getting Ready to Lead *Equipped to Serve*

Chapter One How to Build an Effective Volunteer Team.........................9

Chapter Two How to Use *Equipped to Serve* 17

SECTION TWO: The *Equipped to Serve* Course

Session One You Are Valuable 21

Session Two Know Your Audience 29

Session Three Hitting Your Target.....................................41

Session Four How to Develop Healthy Relationships with Teens 51

Session Five How to Lead a Small Group...61

Session Six Caring Skills 101..73

SECTION THREE: Resources

Appendix A Sample Volunteer Youth Worker Job Descriptions..............84

Appendix B Sample Volunteer Application Form..................................86

Appendix C Interest and Skill Survey 90

ACKNOWLEDGEMENTS

I am grateful to my wife, Sue, who has been with me through the journey of youth ministry, and to my staff at Youth Leadership, who are superb co-workers.

My passion to train volunteers and my belief in their value comes from a caring adult who had the courage to step out of his world and meet for breakfast with a confused teenager. And so, this book is dedicated to a simple man named Bob Hagstrom. Thanks Bob.

Dennis "Tiger" McLuen

INTRODUCTION

As a young college student, I was recruited into a youth ministry career that has continued over the past twenty-one years. The only problem was that I thought I was only agreeing to help out on Tuesday nights! I didn't know what I was getting into, didn't have any training, and wasn't really prepared for the task. The amazing thing is that despite my inadequacies, God has worked with me and I have thoroughly enjoyed the journey.

These past years have now come full circle. I began as a volunteer, worked part-time in youth ministry, and then spent over twelve years as a full-time youth worker who was always looking for new volunteer recruits. Now, I teach others about youth ministry and volunteer in my church. What goes around, comes around.

This book is designed to motivate, equip, and train adult volunteers in youth ministry. We want to assist your ministry to teenagers by helping you develop your adult volunteer leaders. I realize that as the leader of a group, *you* may be in any number of situations—full-time, part-time, or even leading as a volunteer. This resource is designed to assist you at whatever level you find yourself. These sessions will begin the process of equipping your adults for more effective ministry to teenagers and will provide a structured time for your adult leadership team to meet and build a sense of common purpose.

Why *Equipped to Serve*?

Youth ministry is a strategic opportunity to share the Good News of Christ to a group of people who are formulating life-long values and decisions. Most churches recognize youth ministry as a high priority for potential members. One study of 553 families found that an effective youth ministry program was a major factor in choosing a church for 80% of them, with 59% citing it as "very important."[1] And yet, we consistently see churches struggle in this area of ministry. The need to address this struggle is at the heart of *Equipped to Serve*.

Youth ministry is more than an opportunity to lead programs for adolescents. It is an awesome responsibility given to the church. When Jesus tells us to bring the little children to him (Mark 10:14), he is not telling us to stop when the children enter junior high school! Churches need to be intentional in their desire to motivate, equip, and train those adults who respond to this call. Author and veteran youth worker Jim Burns suggests that "the most important but overlooked aspect of youth ministry is building a dynamic youth staff. . . . The quality and quantity of any youth ministry program directly depends on the adult involvement in the program."[2] *Equipped to Serve* is designed to equip your adult leadership team to be more effective in its ministry to teenagers.

We believe in the power of caring adults involved in the lives of teenagers. We believe that significant things can happen in your church and community because you are willing to take the time to build a bridge of friendship to teenagers. That bridge can be the tool God uses to bring healing and wholeness to a broken life. It can be the way a young person first hears about Jesus. It can be a place of reconciliation. We believe this training program will help you and your team of leaders accomplish these goals for the teenagers in your church and community.

chapter one

How to Build an Effective Volunteer Team

I once did a major remodeling project on my house. To put it politely, I was a bit overconfident in my building skills. Even though I had never tackled such a large project, I jumped into this one and soon realized I was in over my head.

As I stood in a large hole in the ground and tried to decide where and how to lay the footings for the new foundation, reality hit home. Even though this work was below ground and would soon be hidden by tons of dirt, I knew that if I messed up here, I would pay the price later. The footings for the foundation would make all the difference in the world. Even nice windows don't look good if the house is crooked or unstable!

In the same way, I believe that what we do "below ground" in youth work makes all the difference in the effectiveness of our ministry. Too many youth ministries focus on the visible things without asking if their foundation is secure.

One of the key foundations of effective youth ministry is developing and equipping adult leaders. We all say that we want adult volunteers in youth ministry, but few of us can explain why, other than that we are too busy and need help. As you prepare to implement *Equipped to Serve*, keep these four foundations for effectively utilizing volunteers in mind:

1. Develop a clear vision for how your volunteers will improve your ministry

What do you hope to accomplish by involving adult volunteers in youth ministry? Without a clear vision of what your volunteers can accomplish, these people simply become a dumping ground for jobs that you don't want.

Dewey Bertolini reminds us that one of the misconceptions about developing a volunteer staff is that the team will lighten our work load. He cautions: "We will never have a light load, no matter how big a staff we may have. We must build a multiple staff with multiple gifts and goals because an effective ministry to teenagers must be multifaceted. Our efforts have nothing to do with getting out from a load of work."[1]

An adult volunteer team provides greater opportunity for teenagers to build relationships with caring, faithful adults who can share God's love in human, concrete terms. Youth ministry provides a unique opportunity for adults to get involved in the lives of teenagers. This vision must drive our efforts in volunteer recruitment and training.

Many of us confuse leadership with the idea that we must do all the jobs in the ministry. Even Moses had to learn that being called into leadership does not mean that one is called into leadership alone. Numbers 11:10-17 illustrates how Moses learned from God that bringing others into leadership in specific roles allowed him to be more effective in his leadership. He complained to God because he felt overwhelmed with the responsibility of leading the nation. He got upset with the tasks that never seemed to end and took up more time than he had to give. Do you ever feel that way?

In verse 11 Moses says, "What have I done to displease you that you put the burden of all these people on me?" He continues with his lamenting and ends with what I think of as the Youth Workers' Prayer:

> "I cannot carry all these people by myself; the burden is too heavy for me. If this is how you are going to treat me, put me to death right now. . . ."

Without a volunteer team, ministry will drive you to this kind of frustration. The needs in your ministry, no matter what size your group, will always exceed your ability to meet those needs. We need to follow Jesus' example and Moses' experience and develop others who will come alongside us in ministry. Share the burden and your ministry will be multiplied.

 ## Benefits of a Volunteer Team

- A volunteer team can develop relationships with kids that you would not be able to reach on your own.

- A volunteer team can model a variety of adult personality styles and faith expressions for your teenagers.

- A volunteer team can manifest the biblical model for team ministry. Although Jesus' mission was to reach out to all people, he spent the majority of his time with his twelve disciples.

- A healthy volunteer team will energize and motivate one another.

- You will be encouraged both by the tasks your volunteers accomplish and the personal support they can provide.

Barriers to Building an Effective Volunteer Team

■ **We're insecure.**
Pastor Greg McKinnon suggests that personal insecurity and pride undermine our ability to build an effective volunteer staff.[2] We either feel like we are imposing on others, or we secretly don't want to share the recognition from the kids or the church.

■ **We see ourselves as Lone Rangers.**
This desire to "do it ourselves" is at the root of many unhealthy volunteer teams. It takes work to recruit, develop, and train a volunteer team. To be effective, we must be committed to a team approach.

■ **We want to control everything.**
We have less control when we give it away to others. Our volunteers may not do the job the same way we would. It may be done differently, or not as well as we would do it— or it may be done even better!

■ **We fail to provide clear roles for our volunteers.**
We can be too vague when utilizing volunteers. Most volunteers will soon tire of the struggle to find out what is expected of them.

■ **We have a shortsighted view of ministry.**
It may seem easier to do it ourselves rather than hassle with finding leaders, training them, supervising them, etc. But if we don't, we're virtually guaranteeing ourselves a short-lived career in youth ministry. We'll just burn out.

2. Learn how to recruit and nurture new volunteers

I was always waiting for the day when people would call me up and ask me to please put them on the waiting list to be on our leadership team. Their experience and enthusiasm would be high, but I wouldn't be able to find a spot for them because of all the other qualified leaders I had. (Ah, but to have a dream!)

Unfortunately, I have never met anyone in youth ministry that has even been close to this fantasy. Adult leaders must be recruited into youth ministry. Recruitment is necessary because our churches are filled with people who may be effective in youth ministry but aren't willing to come forward on their own. An effective youth worker is aware that some adults are simply afraid of teenagers. They see them as unmanageable or threatening, and feel unprepared for such a task. I've worked with many adults with good leadership skills who at first did not consider themselves candidates for youth ministry because of an idealized "image" they had of what an effective volunteer leader should be like. We need to help these people understand that youth ministry is a valid opportunity for them.

People are best recruited to a vision, not just a job. Help your recruits see their responsibilities as a means to an end, not an end in themselves. Present your vision of youth ministry and why volunteer leaders are needed. As you present your case, keep these seven recruiting tips in mind:

Clearly outline your expectations.

Be honest about the job expectations, time demands, and responsibilities. It isn't that we intentionally lie, but we often want leaders so badly that we minimize the responsibilities.

Develop job descriptions for your leaders that summarize expectations and provides estimates of how much time it will take to fulfill their particular responsibilities. (You can find samples of volunteer youth leader job descriptions on pages 84-85.)

Create a variety of opportunities.

Provide a wide variety of opportunities with varying time commitments. Adults are busy, and the old model of all leaders giving the same amount of time per week doesn't work in most churches. Providing a variety of jobs can widen the pool of potential adult volunteers you can draw from.

Recruit people with a variety of gifts, talents, and interests.

Build a three-dimensional leadership team. God can use a diverse group of adults to reach out to the diverse group of young people in your church and community.

Give recruits time to consider your request.

Youth ministry is not the kind of commitment you want to press on people. They should have time to think, pray, talk with their spouses if they are married, and consider the cost. It is better to be thoughtfully turned down than to bring in a hasty recruit who drops out three months later. Set a specific time when you will contact people for their answers.

Ease your new volunteers into service.

Ease your new volunteers into leadership with this simple model for training and development:

I DO—YOU WATCH ....(Observed Leadership)

I DO—YOU DO ....(Shared Leadership)

YOU DO—I WATCH ....(Trained Leadership)

YOU DO—I GO DO SOMETHING ELSE...............(Owned Leadership)

This process helps you to avoid the most common mistake in leadership development: prematurely dumping a job on an unprepared new recruit. This model allows time to train and develop your volunteer.

The time needed to work through this process can be different for each volunteer. Some adults can move to owned leadership in a relatively short time, while others will take longer. There are also many good volunteers who have no desire to function at the owned leadership level.

Be positive, personal, and persistent.

Positive means you are not using guilt as a club to get people to take the jobs you want filled. Rather, think about what you are excited about in your youth ministry that you can share with potential leaders. What are the benefits and "payoffs" you can share?

Personal means that you don't approach recruits generically. Talk to potential volunteers face-to-face. Tell them specifically why you feel that *they* would provide a distinct benefit to the kids in your group. It's time consuming, but it's worth it.

Persistent means that you always have your eyes and ears open for people who may fit on your leadership team and who have gifts that can be developed.

Conduct personal background checks on every potential volunteer.

As uncomfortable as it may be, develop a background check system for all potential volunteers. Ask specific, probing questions in your oral interviews; secure written statements from your recruits in the application form. You may want to require job references or even a criminal record check. There are various state laws that affect churches and volunteers who work with children or teenagers. Check with other churches and social service agencies to see what kind of systems they utilize. Also, consult professional legal counsel and call your denominational

Ideas for Recruiting New Volunteers

Advertise.
Although this is the least effective, it still is needed. It does more than recruit, because it also gets the word out about the needs in your youth ministry program.

Ask current volunteers for names.
Current volunteers know what is expected, are invested in the future of the program, and have ideas on who would work well with teenagers. Having *them* ask these people to consider becoming involved can be very effective.

Ask your kids for their suggestions.
The list may surprise you, and when you share this information with the selected adults they might be surprised as well. At the minimum, it is an affirmation to the chosen adults and a statement to the youth that you want to listen to them. Oftentimes, it also connects you with an excellent leader! Have your teens contact these adults to let them know that they ended up on this list. The teens could invite them to consider becoming involved; then you can follow up and go over the specific expectations.

Talk to your senior pastor.
He or she may be a good source for potential recruits, and keeping him or her informed about your youth ministry is an important part of a healthy professional relationship.

Develop an Interest and Skill Survey.
Survey adults in your church regarding their interests and willingness to provide help and resources for the youth ministry program. You may find people who are willing to help out in a variety of ways. (You can find a sample Interest and Skill Survey on pages 90-91.)

Expose your church to the youth ministry and the kids involved.
Opportunities such as youth Sundays and mission trip presentations are places where the seeds of recruitment can be planted.

How to Keep Your Volunteers Motivated

Keep them involved.

Volunteers need to feel that they are involved in the shaping of the ministry and that their involvement makes a distinct contribution, whether it's up front or behind the scenes.

Communicate your vision of the ministry.

A good leadership team knows your vision and is energized by the "why" behind the "what."

Encourage, support, and affirm.

People need an environment in which they sense encouragement. An affirmed youth ministry team is a motivated team.

Build community.

Provide regular times for volunteers to share about the ministry, about teenagers, and about their struggles with one another. Also, build in times for your volunteers to just have fun together!

Give them permission to quit.

Offer a specific term of service. There are different ideas about the length of that term, but I recommend one school year as the minimum. Make it clear that when their term is completed, they are free to leave without guilt.

Give them equal measures of responsibility and authority.

Allow your volunteers to participate in decision making. Effective youth ministries will offer volunteers responsibility and authority in equal measures.

Support them when they're discouraged.

Give your volunteers permission to talk about their struggles with discouragement—not just to complain, but to help them to move past their feelings.

Give them honest feedback and sincere recognition.

Conduct regular feedback and evaluation sessions with your volunteers. Good leadership development also recognizes work well done. You can do this in formal ways (such as recognition dinners, plaques, and certificates) as well as informal ways (through conversations or spontaneous words of support).

office to see if they have a recommended procedure or form that you can use. (You can find a sample Volunteer Application Form on pages 86-89.)

3. Develop your volunteers

Adults need more than a willingness to work with teenagers— they need basic training and a supportive team atmosphere. Training is not just dispensing information to a group of people; it's helping people develop into men and women who are more effective in their ministry to teenagers.

As you develop your volunteer leaders, be clear about what kinds of people you are looking for. The old acronym F.A.T. suggests that you should look for people who are:

> **F**aithful
> **A**vailable
> **T**eachable

Although simple (*and* venerable), this acronym sets the tone for what is needed in your adult leaders. It is important that they are faithful both to Christ and to the youth ministry. They need to be available and ready to commit a portion of their availability to the youth ministry. And finally, they need to have a teachable spirit. They should see themselves as both teacher and student, leader and follower.

As your volunteers learn and grow, they will begin to exhibit characteristics that will identify them as effective adult volunteers. While not an exhaustive list, the following characteristics are the kinds of traits you want to see in your volunteer team:

- Good listening skills
- Empathy for teen perspectives on life
- Enjoyment of teenagers
- Solid spiritual, emotional, and relational foundations in their own lives
- Patient, flexible, and affirming
- Perseverent
- Principled, but not judgmental
- Understanding of appropriate roles with teenagers
- Good relational skills
- A sense of humor
- Dependable

Set specific standards for leaders in your youth ministry. While your staff can be made up of people with various gifts, abilities, and personality styles, it shouldn't be open to just anyone. The quality of your ministry will depend upon your ability to develop, articulate, and positively enforce your standards for what constitutes a qualified volunteer youth worker.

4. Be sensitive to your volunteers' needs

The volunteers on your team need to have some of their own needs addressed in order to remain motivated. An effective team will have ways that the members feel like they get "paid." Ideas like those outlined on page 14 can help meet the valid needs of your volunteer staff.

While recruiting and nurturing your volunteers is a constant (and sometimes daunting) part of your job, it is the key to effective ministry. A consistent stream of willing and teachable adult volunteers is the lifeline you'll need to stay effective — and sane — in youth ministry. ⊕

chapter two

How to Use
Equipped to Serve

E*quipped to Serve* is a six-session training program designed to help you to equip adults who will have some leadership role with your teenagers. Each session is designed to take between forty-five and ninety minutes, and includes brief video segments to support the course material.

What *Equipped to Serve* Will Enable You to Do
■ Encourage volunteers in the valuable role they can play in the lives of teenagers
■ Help volunteers gain insight into teenagers as well as identify specific characteristics of the teenagers in your church
■ Help your leadership team identify and articulate your goals for ministry
■ Help your volunteers develop necessary skills for effective ministry to teenagers
■ Help build community among your leadership team
■ Increase the motivation of your volunteers
■ Help your volunteers develop specific action steps to improve their ministry to teenagers

What *Equipped to Serve* Is Not
Equipped to Serve is not all you need to know about youth ministry. And *Equipped to Serve* is not the only ministry resource you will ever need. It only covers training adult leaders for ministry to teenagers. I am not addressing the unique contribution that teens themselves can make to your ministry. There are many peer ministry resources available that complement what I cover here. (I recommend *Peer Counseling* and *Advanced Peer Counseling* by Joan Sturkie and Dr. Siang-Yan Tan, available from Youth Specialties.)

Finally, *Equipped to Serve* will not do all your work for you. This is not *Six Easy Steps to Effective Youth Ministry*. (Frankly, I don't think there *are* six easy steps!) You will still need to recruit and supervise your volunteer staff and facilitate these sessions. You are an important part of the leadership team, and I hope to work with you to build up your ministry to these adults.

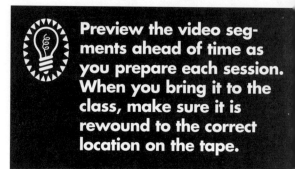

Preview the video segments ahead of time as you prepare each session. When you bring it to the class, make sure it is rewound to the correct location on the tape.

Who Should Attend?

This course is designed primarily for adults who already have some interest and/or involvement in your youth ministry program. However, these sessions can be effective with any adults who may be considering working with teenagers but haven't yet made a commitment. Participation in these sessions may be just what they need to make their decision.

Leading *Equipped to Serve*

This course does not require you to be a youth ministry expert or have special training or expertise. The Leader's Guide, video, and Volunteer Handbook contain all the materials necessary for you to lead effective training meetings for your volunteer leaders.

Your role in leading *Equipped to Serve* includes:

■ Making everyone feel welcome, comfortable, and part of the group. Use your own style to create a climate of comfort.

■ Introducing and explaining the topic for each session.

■ Showing the video. If you don't know how to operate a VCR, have someone else do it. If you have access to a large-screen monitor or a video projection system, use it. It is important that everyone is able to clearly see and hear the video.

■ Facilitating the discussions. Help your volunteers to interact with each other and honestly share their reactions and ideas.

■ Pacing the meeting. You will need to determine how much time to spend on each aspect of the meeting in order to finish within the time limit you have set.

You will need sixty to ninety minutes to cover the material for each session. If you wish to take care of other matters during this time (such as prayer, program planning, brainstorming, etc.) you'll need to allow additional time. If at all possible, hold your *Equipped to Serve* sessions independent of other agenda.

■ Bringing closure to each session. Allow time to bring each session to a point of resolution. That doesn't mean that every question has to be answered or that every problem has to be resolved. But there does need to be a sense of finality and closure following each session. Have your volunteers share what important things they've learned or what they plan to do as a result of the session. Keep your eye on the clock in order to have a strong closing to the meeting.

■ Promoting this training course to your volunteers. Get the word out about this series, and personally invite your potential leaders to ensure the highest possible attendance.

How to Present *Equipped to Serve*

This training course is designed to be presented in six successive meetings. However, *Equipped to Serve* can also be used as part of a volunteer staff retreat before the school year begins. Sessions One through Three could be used to focus the team on the upcoming year. Sessions Four through Six could form the basis for your first meetings in the fall.

You can find an outline for a complete staff training weekend in *Great Retreats for Youth Groups*, available from Youth Specialties. With a few modifications, you can plug in the material from *Equipped to Serve* to replace the content portions of the retreat outline. (*Great Retreats for Youth Groups* also contains twelve additional retreat outlines for youth ministry. For order information, call toll-free 1-800-776-8008.)

Author's Note

This course is a tool I have designed to assist you in your ministry. I pray that God will use it to encourage you and make your volunteer team stronger in more effective in their ministry. Enjoy this time together, and may God bless you and your leadership team.

Dennis "Tiger" McLuen

You Are Valuable

SESSION ONE

You Are Valuable

ESTIMATED TIME: 45-60 minutes

This session encourages your volunteers to see how God can use them in youth ministry. They will look back at influential people in their lives, and then use that perspective to look ahead to the opportunities they have to influence young people in your youth group.

BIG IDEAS

■ People are a vital link God uses to communicate to teenagers.
■ The adult volunteer serves as a link between God(the abstract)and the teenager (the concrete).
■ Imperfect people are qualified for ministry.

SESSION BENEFITS

■ Each adult will be reminded of people who impacted them as a teen.
■ Each participant will see that the qualities their influential people modeled are ones that they can offer to kids today.
■ Each volunteer will be motivated to see beyond their imperfections and fears and envision their potential to effectively minister to youth.

MATERIALS NEEDED

■ Whiteboard or easel with markers
■ VCR and monitor
■ *Equipped to Serve* video, cued to segment number one
■ Pens or pencils for each volunteer
■ Volunteer Handbook for each volunteer

RELEVANT SCRIPTURE

Colossians 1:7: *"You learned [the gospel] from Epaphras, our dear fellow servant..."*

SESSION OUTLINE

Introduction (5-10 minutes)

Welcome the group and introduce your format (e.g., weekly meetings, weekend retreat, etc.). Say something like, "My goals for our time together are both to teach you about youth ministry and to help you become a part of our youth ministry team."

Next, have people introduce themselves. Depending on your style, you can use *Let's Get Acquainted, The Name Game,* or your own get-acquainted activity.

Let's Get Acquainted

Have your volunteers fill out Worksheet 1.1 (found on page 27 of your Leader's Guide and page 11 of the Volunteer Handbook). When they've completed their worksheets, come back together and have everyone share their answers (and some laughs). Keep it light and easy.

The Name Game

Have each leader, one at a time, give his or her first name and an adjective that describes how he or she is feeling about youth ministry. The adjective must begin with the same letter as the person's first name, and then becomes the person's "title." For example, Terry might be "Tentative Terry" because he is unsure and a little afraid. Jane might be "Juiced-up Jane" because she is excited. The second person introduces the first person's title, and then gives their own. The third person introduces the first two, then himself or herself, and so on.

Small Groups (10 minutes)

Now, break your volunteers into smaller groups of three to five persons each. Have these groups complete Worksheet 1.2 (found on page 28 of your Leader's Guide and page 12 of the Volunteer Handbook), then share their answers and comments together in their groups.

Have one person in each small group record the answers to question four. When they've finished, reconvene the large group. Have each group recorder share the collected fears and worries about youth ministry as you list them on your whiteboard or easel.

LEADER HINT

Be ready to add some of the most commonly-shared fears and anxieties, including:

- Feeling inadequate for the task
- Worried about being undertrained
- Concerned that they can't relate to teenagers
- Unclear what is expected of them

Video Segment Number One (6 minutes)

Lead into the video by saying something like, "We share a lot of common fears and worries about working with youth. This is why I think this training series is so important. This material will help you to feel more comfortable in your leadership role. It will also help us get to know each other better, so we can support and encourage one another as a team. Let's begin by watching this video segment."

When the video is finished, make the transition with a statement like, "Tiger and Mike both suggest that youth ministry is often done by people like Epaphras—ordinary people who are used by God to touch lives. Let's take a look back and recall the people that helped us along as we were growing up."

Influential People (10-15 minutes)

Ask your volunteers to describe people who influenced their lives as teenagers who were not members of their immediate families. As people share the names of their mentors, also have them describe the roles the mentors played in their lives (i.e., teacher, best friend, counselor, etc.). Record these names and a one-word description of the roles on your whiteboard or easel.

OPTION

Break back into your small groups for this sharing exercise, then reconvene and have your small groups share their findings with the whole group.

LEADER HINT

Some of your volunteers may not be able to name any such adult. Give them time to sensitively explore their feelings as they work through this realization.

Next, have your group share one- or two-word phrases that describe the *qualities* or *characteristics* of their mentors. List these qualities and characteristics on your whiteboard or easel.

Now say something like, "As we look at these people who influenced us as kids, and look at the characteristics we remember, we can see that they were often ordinary people like you and me. What made them influential was not necessarily that they were superbly gifted or extraordinarily talented—it was their personal interest in our lives that communicated authentic caring."

LEADER HINT

Save your lists of mentors and their qualities for Session Four. This will help you to remind your volunteers that influential relationships with teenagers are achievable. Young people are not looking for mentors with particular skills, but people with caring qualities.

Video Segment Number Two (4 minutes)

Make the transition into this video segment by saying something like, "As we've already discussed, all of us have fears as we prepare to work with kids. It is natural, but we're here because youth ministry is a great place to serve. As we watch this second video segment, let's focus on how God can use us in kids' lives this year."

Small Groups (5-10 minutes)

When the video segment is finished, break back into your small groups to discuss the following questions:

■ What did you hear in this video segment that addressed some of the fears we have talked about?

■ How do you feel about the opportunities you can have to touch kids' lives through our youth ministry?

Prayer (5 minutes)

End your session with a time of prayer for the youth ministry. Have your volunteers pray in their small groups, then close the time for the whole group. Admit your fears and acknowledge that God can use your ordinary team to touch kids in extraordinary ways with the good news of the Gospel. 🌐

Author's Note

Your team may not be large enough to break into smaller groups when called for in the Sessions. That's okay! Just stay together and conduct the various activities as one unit.

Let's Get Acquainted

1 Describe yourself, your situation in life (married, single, etc.) and what you do (work, school, etc.).

2 What do you like to do best with your free time?

3 When you play competitive games (from Monopoly to sports), you usually:
- a. Get bored
- b. Get into an argument
- c. Cheat
- d. Hang in there to the bitter end
- e. Have fun no matter what
- f. Win at all costs

4 Share a favorite childhood vacation memory:

5 Why did you come to this meeting?
- a. I was asked to come and couldn't say no
- b. I have friends who are here
- c. I am curious
- d. I have past experience in youth ministry
- e. I want to help the youth
- f. I'm not sure
- g. Other: _____

Fears and Worries: Past and Present

Complete this sheet, then share your answers and comments with the others in your group.

1 **Write down two or three fears or worries that you had as a junior higher:**

2 **What is one accomplishment you achieved as a teenager that you feel good about?**

3 **On the following scale, put an X to mark your "worry quotient" as an adolescent:**

| No worries | Pretty relaxed | Up and down | High tension |

4 **What are some of your fears or worries as you think about working with young people this year in youth ministry?**

Know Your Audience

SESSION TWO

Know Your Audience

ESTIMATED TIME: 55-75 minutes

This session provides your volunteers a brief orientation to teenage qualities and characteristics. They'll have the opportunity to identify different categories of teenagers in your church; then, together, you'll examine the needs of each group and discuss specific strategies to minister to each group.

BIG IDEAS

■ Effective leaders know their audience *generally* (characteristics and developmental information) as well as *specifically* (individual teenagers in the group).

■ A leadership team talks together about the individual teenagers who are a part of their ministry in order to target their ministry.

■ Categorizing teenagers can help us become more effective in reaching those teenagers for Christ.

SESSION BENEFITS

■ Each volunteer will know where to turn for more detailed information about normal adolescent development.

■ Each volunteer will be encouraged to consider the specific teens in his or her ministry.

■ Each volunteer will be able to better understand the needs and issues of each category of adolescent.

MATERIALS NEEDED

■ Whiteboard or easel with markers
■ VCR and monitor
■ *Equipped to Serve* video, cued to segment number three

- Pens or pencils for each volunteer
- Volunteer Handbook for each volunteer

RELEVANT SCRIPTURE

Acts 17:19b-20: *They said, "This is a new one on us. We've never heard any-thing quite like it. Where did you come up with this anyway? Explain it so we can understand"* (The Message New Testament in Contemporary English).

SESSION OUTLINE

Introduction (5-10 minutes)

Welcome the group to session two. Say something like, "As adults, we often get 'Adolescent Alzheimer's' disease and forget about our own teenage years. This session will help us do some strategic thinking about the teens we minister to."

Now, break your volunteers into groups of four or five persons each and have them introduce themselves to one another as if they were in the eighth grade. They are to do the introductions in the first person (e.g., "I am Joe, and I am in the 8th grade at Oakview Junior High . . . ") and tell where they go to school, where they live, what they look like, about their families, what activities they are involved in, and what interests they have.

Identifying Your Audience (5 minutes)

Refer your volunteers to Resource Sheet A (found on page 35 of your Leader's Guide and page 19 of the Volunteer Handbook). Say something like, "Now that we've reviewed some memories of our own teen years, we've recognized that adolescents are in a special developmental phase of their lives. This sheet helps us to identify some characteristics of our 'audience'."

Briefly review the characteristics with your group.

LEADER HINT

If you have an overhead projector, make a transparency of Resource Sheet A and display it while you're reviewing the information.

Individual Reflection (5 minutes)

Next, have your volunteers complete Worksheet 2.1 (found on pages 36-37 of your Leader's Guide and pages 20-21 of the Volunteer Handbook) to help your volunteers assess their understanding of the teenage world.

Group Reflection (10-15 minutes)

If your group is large, break into groups of four to five persons each. Have each group share their answers to questions one through three. Then give your volunteers more time to discuss and react to questions four through seven. If your group is smaller, you can do this discussion together.

Conclude the discussion by saying something like, "Understanding the teenage world is an ongoing process that we all need to work at. These teens live in a different world than we do, and a different one than the one we lived in when we were their age. Teenagers are in transition, and are developing their own identity. They face a great deal of influence from a lot of sources. Too many are losing hope. We are all involved in youth ministry because we want to help. One important way to do that is to continue to listen to them and learn about their world. If we listen well enough, we will find creative ways to communicate the Gospel to them."

Video Segment Number Three (8 minutes)

Lead into the video by saying something like, "We can become more effective in listening to teens as we discover their core needs. Identifying various 'categories' of teenagers can also help us to better understand what teens are like and what some of their issues are. This video segment will help us to begin that process."

Assessing Your Audience

When the video segment is finished, introduce this next exercise by saying something like, "In the video segment, Tiger discussed the idea of identifying categories of teenagers—not to box kids in with labels, but to help us to be more aware of the various kinds of kids we serve. We're now going to spend some time as a leadership team looking at the specific kinds of teenagers that we serve. We're going to use Worksheet 2.2 as a way to look at the needs of the various types of teenagers that Tiger mentioned in the video."

Individual Reflection (5-10 minutes)

Have your volunteers complete Worksheet 2.2 (found on pages 38-39 of your Leader's Guide and pages 22-23 of the Volunteer Handbook).

Group Reflection (10-15 minutes)

Bring your group together to share and discuss their answers to Worksheet 2.2. Depending on the size of your leadership team, you can break into smaller groups, or group your volunteers into their responsibility areas. Keep tabs on the discussions to keep them in focus and to fill in gaps for those who had difficulty categorizing kids and identifying needs.

LEADER HINTS

■ New volunteers might not be able to identify categories or kids, but they will benefit from this conversation. Be sure to include them.

■ Give a list of the kids in your youth group to each volunteer.

Conclusion (5 minutes)

Say something like, "Categorizing young people is not meant to stereotype them, but rather to help us identify the needs they have. Asking questions without easy answers can be frustrating at times, but it will help us stay focused as a leadership team. Our youth ministry can't do all things, but we can use our strengths to reach those kids that God gives us. Our effectiveness begins by each of us focusing on knowing the needs of our audience. This session has helped us to begin this process."

Close the meeting by praying for the various categories of young people, for greater clarity in understanding their needs, and for providing healthy ways to address those needs. You could break your volunteers into five groups and have each group pray for one of the five categories of teens and the specific youth within that category. Another option is to use Worksheet 2.2 as a prayer focus. 🜚

LEADER HINT

For further information on adolescent development,
encourage your volunteers to read:
Junior High Ministry (Revised Edition) by Wayne Rice, 1987,
Youth Specialties/Zondervan
Effective Youth Ministry by Roland Martinson, 1988,
Augsburg Publishing House
Too Old, Too Soon by Doug Fields, 1991, Harvest House

The Adolescent Audience— A People Who Are:

■ **In transition—physically, emotionally, socially, mentally, spiritually**
Teens are moving from childhood to adulthood in *all* areas of their lives.

■ **Under influence**
From the media, music, parents, school, peers, the future, and the changing world.

■ **Developing an identity**
Teens desire to gain their own identity separate from parents, teachers, and churches.

■ **Relational in perspective**
The world of the teenager is oriented around relationships or the lack of relationships.

■ **Struggling with their families**
Many teens struggle with how their lives intersect (or collide) with those of their families'.

■ **Changing the way they think**
Teens operate in a visual world and seek immediate results and connections.

■ **Reflecting adult society**
Teenagers often mirror our adult culture back to us in painful ways.

■ **Losing hope**
Growing numbers of teens are feeling more and more hopeless.

■ **Feeling driven**
The average teen can be a roller coaster of emotions.

Know Your Audience

How well do you know the teenage world? Let's find out.

Circle your answers:

1   When I think about the "teenage world," I feel like:
   a. A visitor from another planet.
   b. I haven't studied for the test in class.
   c. I can recognize a teenager.
   d. I know some basic information about adolescence.
   e. I should be teaching this session.

2   In terms of knowing specific teens:
   a. I don't even know where the youth room is.
   b. I don't know any teenagers on a first-name basis.
   c. I know a few kids in this church.
   d. I have a pretty good sense of the kids in this ministry and some of their issues.
   e. I hang out with kids all the time and scare my adult friends.

3   When it comes to knowing teenage culture:
   a. I am clueless—I don't know MTV from M&M's.
   b. I lost touch sometime after the disco craze.
   c. I can recognize the music as I scan by it on my car radio.
   d. I am up on it, but it usually is going by me too quickly.
   e. I am young, hip, and groovy. I know all the lingo and can really connect with kids.

Now, write your answers to the following:

4 **How can I find out more about the world of the teenager?**

5 **How can I get to know some specific teenagers in this church?**

6 **How do I see culture affecting the teenagers in our church and community?**

7 **How do I see the basic needs to be loved, to be valuable, and to be connected expressed in the teenagers in this church?**

Categories of Teenagers

Think about the teenagers in this church or ministry, and the needs that they may have. We will use the categories described on the video to help us to think together about the audience. The definitions of each of these categories are explained on page 39 of this Worksheet. If you have a particular area of responsibility (Sunday school, small groups, etc.) then use this Worksheet for your area only.

Category of teen	Teens who may fit here	Possible needs of these teens
Uninterested		
Attending Resister		
Status Quo		
Seeker		
Committed		

Uninterested

These teenagers are not interested in spiritual things. They usually don't attend youth activities and may be cynical about such things. These young people have questions about life and faith, but tend to think that church and the Bible have no connection to their world.

Attending Resister

These teenagers do attend some or all of your activities, but are there under duress. They are usually pressured to come by their parents and they have little interest in what is happening in the youth ministry. They may be passive in their resistance (apathy, non-involvement) or they may be active (negative, interrupting, sarcastic).

Status Quo

These teens attend youth activities, and may in fact be very consistent. They react with a variety of levels of enthusiasm to the activities, but the key issue for these adolescents is that they do not want church, God, or the Bible to affect their lives in significant ways. Their primary goal in life is to stay the same as the rest of their friends. All adolescents demonstrate this quality at various times, but these teens are focused in not wanting to change. They state belief in God, but have no interest in anything that may challenge them.

Seeker

These teens are starting to ask questions and seek out spiritual things. They are more attentive in class and may talk to you individually. Their attendance may not be consistent, depending on their families, and what category they were in before entering this stage. Yet these adolescents are open to wondering what a life lived for God would look like.

Committed

These teens are serious about their faith and are trying to live it out in their world. They are at different levels of Bible knowledge, and have a variety of personality types, but these teens want to live for God. They can get bored with pat answers, with being spectators, and with having no leadership roles. They want to try new things, be stretched, and get involved.

Hitting Your Target

SESSION THREE

session three

Hitting Your Target

ESTIMATED TIME: 70-90 minutes

This session provides your volunteers an opportunity to share their goals for the youth ministry program. It also allows them to look at the program as a tool to accomplish these goals.

BIG IDEAS

- Vision drives effective youth ministry.
- Programming is a means to an end, not an end in itself.
- An effective volunteer team develops clear, achievable goals.

SESSION BENEFITS

- Each volunteer will develop specific goals for his or her involvement in the youth ministry program.
- The volunteer team will share personal and group goals.
- Every volunteer will understand how programming serves as a tool to achieve ministry goals.
- Each volunteer will be motivated to use the programming window he or she is involved in to accomplish ministry goals.

MATERIALS NEEDED

- Whiteboard or easel with markers or overhead projector and screen
- VCR and monitor
- *Equipped to Serve* video, cued to segment number four
- Pens or pencils for each volunteer
- Volunteer Handbook for each volunteer

RELEVANT SCRIPTURE

Philippians 3:13-14: *" . . . one thing I do: Forgetting what is behind and straining toward what is ahead, I press on toward the goal to win the prize for which God has called me heavenward in Christ Jesus."*

SESSION OUTLINE

Introduction (5-10 minutes)

Welcome your volunteers back and briefly review where you are in the program. The first session discussed fears about youth ministry and how God can use ordinary people to reach teenagers. You then looked in Session Two at the value of knowing your audience.

To introduce this session, say something like, "The key to effective ministry is not to be superhuman, but to be ordinary people with vision. We need to learn how to aim for a valid target in our youth ministry. To do that, we're going to talk about goals for our youth ministry program. Let's begin by looking at a time when you had a goal."

Now break into small groups. Have the groups share times when they were growing up that they established a goal, identified a target and worked toward achieving that goal. Goals could include: saving enough money to buy a toy, attending a camp, earning A's in school, finding a part-time job, etc. Have them share their goals and how it felt when they achieved those goals.

Video Segment Number Four (8 minutes)

When the discussions have concluded, bring everyone back together and say something like, "Goals are targets that can motivate us. For Paul, it was always to focus on the ministry that Christ had given him. He was consumed by it. Before we look at some ideas for setting a target in our youth ministry program, let's begin by watching this video segment that will introduce some of the ideas for our discussion."

Individual Reflection (10 minutes)

After showing the video segment, have your volunteers complete Worksheet 3.1 (found on pages 47-48 of your Leader's Guide and pages 31-32 of the Volunteer Handbook). This Worksheet will help your volunteers apply the information seen on the video, and will prepare them for the discussion of programming as a means to achieve these goals. Before they fill out the Worksheet, say something like, "Setting goals is not an idle exercise but an important step for each of us. We will all benefit if we can clarify what we would like to accomplish in youth ministry and what we would like to see happen with our young people. Let's all fill

LEADER HINT

If your ministry has a mission statement and/or specific goals, share them here.

out Worksheet 3.1 in order to discover what each of us would like to see happen in this youth ministry."

Group Reflection (10-15 minutes)

Using Worksheet 3.1 as the building block for conversation, have your volunteers share their ideas, dreams, and hopes in each of the **Know**, **Do**, **Experience**, and **Become** categories. List these categories on a whiteboard or newsprint, and record your volunteers' ideas as they are shared.

LEADER HINTS

■ This list of goals is not meant to overwhelm the group. No group can do everything on their dream list. Share this observation with your group to help them to see this process as a way to get a sense of the dreams of your group, rather than a guilt-producing list.

■ There will be a variety of perspectives shared during this session. Allow for disagreement and a diversity of suggestions.

Programming Windows (5 minutes)

Move the discussion from the brainstorming of ideas to the main idea of programming as a tool you can use to get at the goals and dreams of youth ministry. Say something like, "The way we can reach some of these goals is to put people and programs together. The video mentioned that we need tools to help us with our programs, and that programs are where the rubber hits the road. Since programs are important, let's learn together about a simple tool to help us look at our programming. It's a Worksheet called 'Programming Windows'."

Individual Reflection (10 minutes)

Now, have your volunteers complete Worksheet 3.2 (found on page 49 of the Leader's Guide and page 33 of the Volunteer Handbook).

Group Reflection (15-20 minutes)

Draw the windows diagram on your whiteboard or newsprint, or display an overhead transparency of the diagram. Have your volunteers share the program ideas they came up with for each of the windows. List these ideas on your chart. Next, take some time to

LEADER HINT

Come prepared with a list of some of the effective programs from the past year or two, and add them if needed.

review the ideas listed. See if you can prioritize the ideas and generate some consensus on which program ideas your ministry team wants to focus on in the upcoming year.

Conclusion and Prayer (5-10 minutes)

Highlight the observations listed on the newsprint or whiteboard for Worksheet 3.1, then lead into your prayer time by saying something like, "Programming is a crucial part of this youth ministry. As the video clip mentioned, all of our programming is a means to an end. We must understand that effective programming should be seen as a tool to achieve a goal. It should use the windows we have, and meet the needs of the teenagers in this ministry. We all have different goals and dreams, and building a balanced program is difficult. We can see the different goals and hopes on our list, and the wide variety of programming options from the windows exercise. Let's pray that the programs we develop will be effective tools that God can use to help us reach kids for Christ." ⚜

Setting Our Ministry Goals

1 What are one or two reactions you have to what Tiger and Mike had to say?

2 What do you think are the benefits to having goals in youth ministry?

3 Now, fill in your personal goals and hopes for the youth ministry program.

Your Ministry Target Area (e.g., Junior high, 10th grade girls, etc.):

_____

I. What would you like your students to KNOW this year?
(e.g., the Bible, family information, denominational doctrine, etc.)

II. What would you like your students to be able to DO this year?
(e.g., skiing, hayrides, progressive dinners, etc.)

III. What would you like your students to EXPERIENCE this year?
(e.g., feeling valued, experiencing worship in a personal way,
being cared for by a peer, etc.)

IV. What would you like them to BECOME this year?
(e.g., able to make healthier decisions, a person more focused on
Christ, etc.)

Programming Windows

This chart will help you look at where (and how) your programs can be placed. Each window is an opportunity to program an event or activity to help you accomplish your goals. These windows are the most common ones, although you may have some variations. It is important to note that each window can impact the others. The things you do in one window may improve, or cause difficulties in, the other windows. For example, a retreat in special events may help you in your Sunday morning window. Using this Programming Windows chart, list some program examples for each window:

Sunday Morning	Midweek Activity
Special Events	**Personal Relationships**

Extra Credit

Go back to Worksheet 2.1. Which categories of teens usually attend certain windows? Do the programs these kids attend meet the needs of those kids? Why or why not?

How to Develop Healthy Relationships with Teens

SESSION FOUR

session four

How to Develop Healthy Relationships with Teens

ESTIMATED TIME: 60-70 minutes

This session provides your volunteers with the motivation and framework to begin to build relationships with the young people in your ministry.

BIG IDEAS

■ Relational ministry clarifies itself in specific, concrete action steps.
■ Volunteers can develop strategies to develop relationships with specific teenagers in their ministry areas.
■ With a limited time budget, the ordinary volunteer can develop healthy relationships with teens.

SESSION BENEFITS

■ Volunteers will see the value of adult/teen relationships.
■ The volunteer team will develop action steps to build relationships with all of the kids who are involved in the youth ministry program.
■ Each volunteer leader will commit a specific amount of time for relational ministry with teens.

MATERIALS NEEDED

■ Whiteboard or easel with markers
■ VCR and monitor
■ *Equipped to Serve* video, cued to segment number five
■ Pens or pencils for each volunteer
■ Volunteer Handbook for each volunteer
■ List of mentors from Session One, rewritten onto a large easel or newsprint sheet

RELEVANT SCRIPTURE

I Thessalonians 2:8: *"We loved you so much that we were delighted to share with you not only the gospel of God, but our lives as well, because you had become so dear to us."*

SESSION OUTLINE

Introduction (10-15 minutes)

Welcome your volunteers to the fourth session. Say something like, "We have looked at how God can use imperfect people like us, and in Session One we spent time remembering people who affected us when we were teens. We have looked at programming as an important part of what we do. Today, we want to look at building healthy relationships with teenagers."

LEADER HINT

Remember to bring the list of mentors and their qualities that you developed in Session One. Rewrite it onto a large newsprint sheet and post it as a reminder of the human dimension to this session. Refer to it as your discussion warrants.

Now break your volunteers into pairs. Have each pair describe healthy relationships they have had with other people. These can be past or present relationships. Have partners answer questions like:

- What made those relationships healthy and productive?
- How did those relationships feel?
- What were the challenges to maintaining those relationships?

When your pairs have finished their discussions, bring the group back together and have a few willing volunteers share what they discussed. List their observations on the whiteboard or newsprint.

Next, read I Thessalonians 2:8 aloud: "We loved you so much that we were delighted to share with you not only the gospel of God, but our lives as well, because you had become so dear to us." Say something like, "Relationships are a crucial part of the life of an adolescent, and we have learned that opportunities for healthy relationships are eroding in our culture. Healthy relationships are a healing part of our ministry, and we want to develop specific action steps we can take as leaders to form healthy relationships with teens."

Video Segment Number Five (5 minutes)

Lead into the video by saying something like, "Since relationships are so crucial to effective youth ministry, this video clip focuses on the concept of relational ministry and offers a working model for each of us to consider."

Individual Reflection (5 minutes)

Now have your volunteers turn to Worksheet 4.1 (found on pages 57-58 in your Leader's Guide and on pages 39-40 in the Volunteer Handbook). Have them read the introduction on personality style differences, and then give the group time for individual response to the video.

Group Reflection (15-20 minutes)

Have your volunteers get into small groups to discuss questions one and two. This will give them the opportunity to share their personality differences and personal reflections about the video clip. Allow about five minutes for this brief reflection, then say something like, "Now, I would like you to do a difficult task: develop your specific relational goals, then share them with one another. As you do, I would like one person in each group to record the goals, *without names*, so we can share them with each other and pray for these goals."

Now, have your volunteers individually complete step three on Worksheet 4.1, then have them share their goals within their groups.

LEADER HINT

Keep yourself available to answer questions and to help individual volunteers who may have difficulty in coming up with their personal ministry goals.

Large Group Reflection (10 minutes)

Bring your group back together and have the recorders for each group share the goals they collected. Write these goals on your whiteboard or easel. Encourage your volunteers as you hear their goals.

LEADER HINTS

■ You can expect a wide range of time commitments and goals. Be sure to affirm everyone's efforts.
■ Some volunteers are very task-focused in their roles. They may have trouble with this exercise, but encourage them to think of even one or two kids they could befriend.

Relationship-Building Tips (5 minutes)

Refer your volunteers to Resource Sheet B (found on page 59 of your Leader's Guide and page 41 of the Volunteer Handbook). Say something like, "Let's face it—initiating relationships with teens is scary for most of us. Let's look at a few tips that

can help us be successful in building healthy relationships with young people."
Briefly review these relationship-building tips with your group.

LEADER HINT

If you have an overhead projector, make a transparency of Resource Sheet B and display it while you're reviewing the information.

Conclusion and prayer (10 minutes)

Say something like, "Building relationships with teens can be challenging, but it is clear that healthy youth ministry depends on adults who get to know teens as people, rather than adults who simply chaperone events. There are a wide variety of ways to be in contact with kids, and of all these different levels of contact work, building relationships is the most important programming window we have. Let's continue to pray for the things we've talked about today and for the relationships that we can develop."

Break your volunteers back into their small groups. Have each group pray for the goals that have been shared and are listed on the whiteboard or easel. Have people encourage one another as they look ahead to building healthy relationships with teenagers.

LEADER HINT

Building relationships with teens is often the most frightening aspect of youth ministry for volunteers. Look out for any opportunity you have to encourage your volunteers in their efforts, and celebrate every small step they take in this area as the important victory that it in fact is.

Relational Ministry on a Busy Schedule

" . . . the foundation of youth ministry is relational ministry, not the ministry of teaching. Where the ministry of teaching is primary, young people will tend to resist it. Where the ministry of friendship is primary, the ministry of teaching can make progress."
Michael Warren, *Youth and the Future of the Church*, 1982, Seabury Press

Each person brings a different personality style to relational ministry. Some of us are energized by groups of people, while others of us prefer quiet, one-to-one relationships. Some of us always follow a plan, while others of us are spontaneous and free-flowing. Some of us state our opinions quickly and easily, while others of us listen more and have difficulty articulating our thoughts.

There is no one right relational style. God wants you to use the personality that he has given you to reach out to teenagers. This Worksheet will help you respond to the idea of relational youth ministry and to the information from Video Segment Number Five.

1 **How do you best get to know others? What style seems to work best for you? Put an X on the line that best fits you when you think of relating to teens:**

Introvert————————————————————————Extrovert
Quiet————————————————————————Noisy
Ask questions————————————————————Give opinions
Behind the scenes————————————————Up front
Planner————————————————————Spontaneous
Homebody————————————————————Let's go out

WORKSHEET 4.1

2 **How have you seen relational ministry work out specifically in your life and the lives of others? (Feel free to include examples from outside youth ministry.)**

3 **Set your personal relational ministry goals, using the formula of one hour and thirty minutes per week given in the video:**

Ten minutes:two phone calls
Twenty minutes:three written notes
One hour:one personal contact—individual or small group

a. Time per week/month I will give to building relationships with teenagers:

b. Specific teens I will focus on in the next six months:

c. Specific steps I will take with those teens:

1.

2.

3.

4.

Note: These specific goals are a way to clarify your hopes and are not meant to weigh you down. If you're having trouble coming up with goals, discuss it with your small group and/or your group leader.

How to Build Healthy Relationships with Teens

- Listen.

- Learn names.

- Show an interest in teens' lives.

- Accept kids as they are.

- Develop a sense of humor.

- Attend events that teens are involved in.

- Initiate, even though it may feel strange.

- Speak naturally and conversationally.

- Be yourself.

- Pray for those kids you are getting to know.

- Communicate your enthusiasm rather than flaunt your doubt.

- Don't force yourself into situations.

- Be prepared to have to earn the right to be heard.

- Be sensitive to boundaries of time, physical contact, emotions, and differences in maturity.

How To Lead A Small Group

SESSION FIVE

session five

How to Lead a Small Group

ESTIMATED TIME: 75-90 minutes
This session introduces the basic skills necessary for leading a small group, and it gives your volunteers an opportunity to practice leading a small group.

BIG IDEAS
- Small-group leadership is a vital part of a volunteer's job description.
- Effective small-group leaders have developed particular attributes and skills.
- Leading small groups is difficult, and volunteers need help and training to be effective small-group leaders.

SESSION BENEFITS
- Your volunteers will understand the value of small-group interaction.
- Each volunteer will learn the skills and attributes needed to lead a small group.
- Each volunteer will observe and/or practice small-group leadership skills.

MATERIALS NEEDED
- Whiteboard or easel with markers
- VCR and monitor
- *Equipped to Serve* video, cued to segment number six
- Pens and pencils for each volunteer
- Volunteer Handbook for each volunteer

RELEVANT SCRIPTURE
Hebrews 10:25: *"Let us not give up meeting together, as some are in the habit of doing, but let us encourage one another — and all the more as you see the Day approaching."*

SESSION OUTLINE

Introduction (5 minutes)

Begin this session by saying something like, "Today's session focuses on leading small groups. All of us probably have been involved in small groups of one kind or another. This session will help us explore the role of leading one of these groups. To begin, let's look at some of our own experiences in small groups."

Individual Reflection (5-10 minutes)

Have each participant complete Worksheet 5.1 (found on pages 67-68 in your Leader's Guide and pages 47-48 in the Volunteer Handbook) individually.

Group Reflection (15 minutes)

When your volunteers have completed Worksheet 5.1, break them into small groups to share their observations about effective and ineffective groups. Designate a recorder in each small group to write down the group's answers to the Worksheet questions.

After your groups have discussed their answers, bring everyone back together and record the observations of the groups on a whiteboard or newsprint. Focus on the observations from question number three, and the fears volunteers shared in question number four.

Video Segment Number Six (8 minutes)

Make the transition to the video by saying something like, "There are many things to think about when leading small groups. This video segment will help us look at some issues we want to be aware of regarding small group leadership."

Application Exercise (15-25 minutes)

When the video segment is completed, say something like, "We all have fears about leading small groups, but small groups are a very helpful part of youth ministry. Let's take some time to practice some of these skills."

Now, break your volunteers into groups of four to five people. One person in each group will facilitate an impromptu discussion on one of the topics listed on Worksheet 5.2 (found on pages 69-70 of your Leader's Guide and on pages 49-50 of the Volunteer Handbook). Say something like, "This exercise will give the leader an opportunity to facilitate a group discussion on one of the topics listed on Worksheet 5.2. Each of you should participate in the discussion, and then we will talk together about this experience."

OPTION

Have the least experienced leader in each group facilitate the discussion.

Group Reflection (10-15 minutes)

When the discussions are finished, have each small group process their experience. Have the participants share what they observed during the group discussion, using Worksheet 5.2 as a guide.

Small-Group Leadership Tips (5-10 minutes)

Refer your volunteers to Resource Sheet C (found on page 71 of your Leader's Guide and page 51 of the Volunteer Handbook). Say something like, "We can all use ideas on how to be more effective small-group leaders. Let's review some helpful tips."

Briefly review these small-group leadership tips with your group.

LEADER HINT

If you have an overhead projector, make a transparency of Resource Sheet C and display it while you're reviewing the information.

Conclusion (10-15 minutes)

Say something like, "Leading small groups can be quite a challenge! It is difficult to ask good questions, listen to group members, and guide the discussion all at the same time. We need to pray for the small group opportunities in our youth ministries and the people who lead them."

Have your volunteers pray for the various small groups in your ministry, and the leaders of those groups.

OPTION

Have all of your volunteers who will be leading small groups in your youth ministry stand and congregate in a group. Then have the rest of your group lay hands on them and pray a prayer of commissioning for these vital small-group leaders.

LEADER HINT

For further training in small-group leadership, encourage your volunteers to read:
A Training Manual for Small Group Leaders, Julie A. Gorman, Victor Books, 1991
Get 'Em Talking, Mike Yaconelli and Scott Koenigsaecker, Youth Specialties/Zondervan, 1990
Teaching the Bible Creatively, Bill McNabb and Steven Mabry, Youth Specialties/Zondervan, 1994

Small-Group Flashback

1 Describe a positive experience you had in a small group as a leader or participant. What was it like? What made the group effective?

2 Now, describe a negative experience you had in a small group as a leader or participant. What was it like?

3 What were the differences between the two groups that made the one group go well and the other one struggle?

4 How do you feel about leading a small group? What do you look forward to? What do you fear?

5 Place an X on the line that reflects your feelings about leading a small-group Bible study/discussion:

| panic-stricken | nervous | fair | pretty relaxed | very cool |

The Small-Group Lab

One person in your small group will be your leader for the next fifteen to twenty minutes. They will lead a discussion on one of the following topics. Please participate fully in the discussion and then record your observations afterwards.

Leader: Facilitate a discussion on one of the topics listed below. Use whatever style feels most comfortable as you get your group to discuss this subject. Stop the group in twenty minutes.

Topics (choose one):

1. Moments when you felt closest to God
2. The joys and struggles of parenting
3. A painful time in your life as a child
4. Why you are involved in youth ministry
5. Some of your goals for life

Participants only complete the following:

1. The leader did the following things to help the discussion:

2. The leader could have been even more effective by:

3. What seemed to be most difficult for the leader?

4. What seemed to be most comfortable for the leader?

5. The leader seemed (place an X on the line):

Nervous _____Comfortable

6. The conversation flowed (place an X on the line):

With difficulty_____Easily

Leader only complete the following:

1. Please mark an X on each scale to indicate how you felt during the exercise:

Nervous _____Calm

Self-conscious _____Focused on group

2. The most difficult part of this exercise was:

3. The part that felt the most comfortable for me was:

4. From this exercise, I learned:

Survival Ideas for Small Groups

(Adapted with permission from *The Youth Builder*, Jim Burns, 1988, Harvest House)

- Include everyone whenever possible.
- At the beginning, get everyone in the group to talk.
- Four in a group is best; six is okay; eight should be the maximum.
- Be aware of new people and include them in the conversation.
- Remember that small groups often raise the tension level (because people can't hide).
- Move from light to heavy discussion.
- Ask "I feel" rather than "I know" questions.
- The longer the group is together, the better they will feel about the group.
- In a small group it's easier to share, pray, encourage, and be personal.
- Prepare your discussion questions and vary how you ask them.
- Avoid any put-downs.
- Discussion questions should be answerable.
- Allow people the right to pass and not share.
- Create a casual and relaxed atmosphere.
- Don't always expound on the answer yourself.
- Call people by name.
- Eye contact and body language are important for the leader.
- When you ask someone to read, make sure he/she is able to read out loud or else don't ask.
- Get your group in a comfortable atmosphere where everyone can see each other's eyes.
- Request confidentiality in the group.

An effective small-group leader:

- Guides the discussion with control and flexibility
- Encourages as much participation as possible
- Asks a variety of questions that involve the group
- Listens well
- Arranges seating to involve participants
- Models the skills he/she wants to develop in group members
- Notices the people in the room, the conversations occurring, and the non-verbal signals
- Creates an inviting, positive atmosphere
- Affirms the ideas expressed by group members
- Doesn't panic with silence
- Doesn't let one person monopolize the discussion

Caring Skills 101

SESSION SIX

session six

Caring Skills 101

ESTIMATED TIME: 65-80 minutes

This session introduces your volunteers to counseling and caring skills needed in youth ministry. The listening exercise provides your volunteers a concrete opportunity to begin to develop skills in caring for teenagers.

BIG IDEAS

■ Listening is the greatest tool in caring for teenagers.
■ There are risks and dangers involved in counseling teenagers.
■ Learning how to refer kids to qualified help, when necessary, is crucial for effective ministry.

SESSION BENEFITS

■ Volunteers will appreciate the value of listening in caring for teenagers.
■ Each volunteer will be able to identify the potential danger areas when counseling teens.
■ Each volunteer will observe and practice active listening skills.
■ Volunteers will be able to identify the three reasons for referral.

MATERIALS NEEDED

■ Whiteboard or easel with markers
■ VCR and monitor
■ *Equipped to Serve* video, cued to segment number seven
■ Pens or pencils for each volunteer
■ Volunteer Handbook for each volunteer

RELEVANT SCRIPTURES

Galatians 6:1: *"Brothers [and sisters], if someone is caught in a sin, you who are spiritual should restore [them] gently. But watch yourself, or you may also be tempted."*

II Corinthians 1:3-4: *"Praise be to the God and Father of our Lord Jesus Christ, the Father of compassion and the God of all comfort, who comforts us in all our troubles, so that we can comfort those in any trouble with the comfort we ourselves have received from God."*

SESSION OUTLINE

Introduction (10 minutes)

Welcome your volunteers to the final session of this training series. Introduce today's subject by saying something like, "This session will address the issue of caring skills needed in youth ministry. We don't intend to turn you into amateur counselors. But the skills you'll learn today will help you be more effective in your listening and caring skills when kids turn to you for help."

Next, break your volunteers into pairs and have them share their answers to the following questions:

- Can you remember a time when you needed to talk to someone?

- What do you remember about that experience?

- Did talking to that person help? Why or why not?

Video Segment Number Seven (6 minutes)

Bring your group back together. Lead into the video by saying something like, "*Counseling* is a word that can convey many different meanings. Today, we want to look at how we can be more effective in listening to and caring for kids who may want to talk to us. Let's begin by watching this video segment."

Discussion (5-10 minutes)

When you've finished watching the video segment, lead a follow-up discussion using the following questions:

- How do you respond to what was shared in the video?

- What concerns do you have about being put in the role of the "counselor"?

Triad Listening Exercise (20 minutes)

Next, move to the Triad Listening Exercise. Say something like, "Listening is the *one* thing we can all offer in our ministry. Listening is both a skill and an attitude.

Many people are ineffective in ministry simply because they don't listen to those who come to them. As listeners, we often follow our own agenda and don't focus our attention on the other person. Good listeners keep their minds open, resist distractions, and are willing to hold their responses to what is being said. It requires hard work to really focus on another person.

"As you begin this exercise, listen for both the content and the feeling the other person shares, and then let the person know you heard him or her by sharing it back to the person. This is not a time to evaluate, give advice, or preach a sermon. This is a time to **listen.**"

Now break your group into triads (threes). One person will share a "problem" with a listener. The third person in the triad will observe the process. This problem needs to be realistic for that person or for a teenager. It may be a current problem in their lives, or one from their past. It may represent the kinds of things that teens have brought to them as a leader, but it shouldn't be a situation that will identify a specific teen in your group.

Some examples of "problems" that could be shared include:

Teen: My mom and dad are fighting a lot; I'm afraid they may get divorced.

Teen: I don't feel accepted by the kids in the youth group.

Adult: I am struggling with whether to put my mom in a nursing home.

The listener will try to discern the content of the problem and the feelings behind the problem. He or she will focus the conversation on the speaker, and will listen actively to the problem. The observer will give feedback on the process. Allow three minutes for each problem, then three minutes for processing. Rotate the roles until everyone has had a chance to participate in all three roles.

Group Reflection (10-15 minutes)

After the triads have finished, bring the groups together for further processing. Facilitate the discussion with the following questions:

■ While you were the "listener," what was the most difficult thing to do?
■ What seemed to work for you?
■ What problems arose?
■ What did you notice when you were the observer?
■ What seemed to help you when you had the problem?
■ What did the listener do to help? What got in the way?

Counseling Skills Review (10 minutes)

Refer your volunteers to Resource Sheets D, E, and F (found on pages 79-81 of your Leader's Guide and pages 56-58 of the Volunteer Handbook). Say something like, "It's impossible to cover all of the information we need to be wise and effective counselors in one brief session. Nonetheless, let's review these Resource Sheets to at least begin the process. I strongly recommend that you go over the information on these Resource Sheets again on your own, and keep them handy for further review throughout the year."

Briefly (but carefully) review these Resource Sheets with your group.

LEADER HINT

If you have an overhead projector, make transparencies of Resource Sheets D, E, and F and display them while you're reviewing this material.

Conclusion and Prayer (5-10 minutes)

Say something like, "Listening and caring are vital parts of our ministry to kids. So is prayer. As we conclude this session and this course, let's pray for our kids and ourselves as we ask God to use us to change teens' lives for the kingdom's sake."

Arrange your group in a circle, holding hands. Begin the time with a brief prayer of thanks for how God has used this training course to further your ministry with kids. When you've finished, squeeze the hand of the person to your left, who then prays. When that person is finished, he or she squeezes the hand of the person to the left, and so on. If anyone desires to pass, he or she simply squeezes the person's hand to the left when it is his or her turn. When the circle returns to you, close the session and the volunteer training course with your prayer.

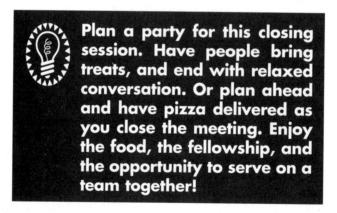

Plan a party for this closing session. Have people bring treats, and end with relaxed conversation. Or plan ahead and have pizza delivered as you close the meeting. Enjoy the food, the fellowship, and the opportunity to serve on a team together!

LEADER HINT

For further training on caring skills, encourage your volunteers to read:
Counseling Teenagers, Dr. Keith Olson, Group Books, 1984
Equipped to Care , William J. Rowley, Ed. D., Victor Books, 1990
Peer Counseling in Youth Groups, Joan Sturkie and Dr. Siang-Yan Tan, Youth Specialties/Zondervan, 1993

The Ministry of Listening

"Everyone should be quick to listen, slow to speak" (James 1:19)

🌐 ATTITUDES in Effective Listening 🌐

Be sincere. Don't try to fake good listening—it won't work. Take the time to listen properly.

Accept the other person and his or her feelings. Good listening begins with acceptance.

Trust in the person's capacity to handle his or her feelings, and have confidence in his or her ability to work at solutions. Trust in the Lord to work with this person.

Active listening does not solve problems. It creates an environment conducive to problem solving.

🌐 GUIDELINES for Effective Listening 🌐

Identify the CONTENT in the message. What is being said? React to what is being presented, not the way it is presented.

Figure out the FEELINGS in the messages. How does the person feel about what he or she is saying? Try to see and feel the situation through that person's eyes, not your own.

FEEDBACK what you are hearing. Do this without judgment or without sending back a message of your own. Share both the content and the feelings that you are hearing.

Try to paraphrase what the other person has said. Condense it down to a sentence or two. Listen for themes that you are observing. Begin your sentences with a short introduction:

> "You feel that . . . "
> "What I am hearing you say is . . . "
> "You're (name the feeling) . . . "
> "So, it's kinda like . . . "

Practice, Practice, Practice

Practice some more!

Counseling and Caring Skills

Five Key Questions for the Helper

1 Why am I here?

2 What do I have to offer this person?

3 What does this person need?

4 What are my limits as a helper?

5 How long can I offer this to this person?

Seven Danger Areas in Counseling

1 **The Question-Answer Trap**
We don't really listen; we just focus on asking questions.
Be careful of how many questions you ask.

2 **The Messiah Complex**
Since the teen has talked to us, we can "rescue" him or her.

3 **The Bible Bullet Syndrome**
We slide into easy answers with a Bible verse tagged on.
Caring for people is bringing them into contact with the Great Physician,
but it is not always filled with easy answers.

4 **The Helping = Fixing Mentality**
If we are to help people, we must fix their problems.

5 **The "Counseling Others to Meet Our Needs" Syndrome**
We care for others in order to meet our own needs. We must not counsel
out of curiosity, a need for power, a need for relationships, or out of guilt.

6 **The No-Weaknesses Weakness**
Every counselor has certain limitations and weaknesses. This is only
dangerous when we won't admit them.

7 **The Boundary Violation**
Our job is to work within the boundaries of other people, and not
impose our expectations on them.

Three Reasons to Refer a Counselee

Time Limits

We don't have the time it takes to work through the issues presented to us.

Competence Limits

The level of expertise needed to deal with the issues presented to us is more than we can offer.

Emotional Limits

The subject or issue presented is inappropriate for us.

See your youth pastor or pastor for a list of local referral sources you can utilize when it's time for you to withdraw from the counseling process.

Equipped to Serve

Resources

APPENDIX A
SAMPLE VOLUNTEER YOUTH WORKER JOB DESCRIPTIONS

A job description identifies the objectives of the position and summarizes what is expected. You may also want to add more general expectations such as building relationships with teens, being a Christian example, and being prepared for the stated tasks. Some job descriptions include what the volunteer can expect from the church and/or the youth minister such as training, being prayed for, and compensation for certain expenses.

Following are two sample job descriptions:

Bible Study Leader—Senior High

Objective
- Lead a weekly Bible study with a group of 4-9 senior high students

Responsibilities
- Use or adapt Bible study curriculum given by youth pastor
- Meet weekly with small group and facilitate the meeting
- Offer one social gathering every quarter for the small group
- Pray regularly for the group members
- Attend training sessions whenever possible

Time Commitment
- 2-3 hours per week for preparation and small group
- Attendance at monthly leaders' meetings
- Occasional involvement in other large-group youth events

Term of Service
- One school year

Responsible to
- Youth pastor

Music Coordinator

Objective
- Lead the music component of the Wednesday night youth group

Responsibilities
- Choose music for the 20-minute worship time
- Meet with the worship team for practice on Saturday mornings
- Lead music on Wednesday night (or find music leader)
- Pray for the members of the worship team
- Attend youth worker training sessions whenever possible

Time Commitment
- 2-4 hours per week for preparation and practice
- Attendance at monthly leaders' meeting

Responsible to
- Youth pastor

APPENDIX B
SAMPLE VOLUNTEER APPLICATION FORM

Dear friend,

Thank you for considering serving in the youth ministry at First Church. I appreciate your willingness to give your time and talents on behalf of young people.

Here at First Church, we are committed to providing a healthy, safe environment for every young person to whom we minister. Therefore, we screen all youth ministry volunteer applicants. This process may feel uncomfortable, and it certainly reflects the fallen world in which we live. We believe, however, that it is imperative to do all we can to ensure a safe environment for all young people. We realize that some of the information we are requesting is personal in nature, and we want you to know that all such information will be held in strict confidence.

If you have any questions, please feel free to contact me. I thank you for your service in the name of Jesus, and I look forward to working with you.

Sincerely in Christ,

YOUTH MINISTRY
VOLUNTEER STAFF APPLICATION
First Church

Name_____Phone _____

Home Address_____Zip _____

Profession/Occupation _____

Education _____

Social Security #:_____ Driver's License #: _____

How long have you attended this church? _____

Personal History

[**Note:** Where necessary, please supply additional information on separate sheets of paper.]

Please list the names and addresses of other churches you have attended regularly during the past five years, noting all previous work involving children and youth and the name of a supervisor for each ministry.

_____

_____

_____

_____

Please list the names and addresses of other youth serving agencies or ministries where you have worked with young people, the role you played, and the name of your supervisor.

_____

_____

_____

_____

Please list your employment during the past five years:

_____

_____

_____

_____

Why are you interested in working with young people?

Have you ever been convicted in a court of law for child abuse or any crime involving actual or attempted sexual molestation?
_____ Yes   _____ No
If yes, please explain (you will be asked to meet with one of the pastoral staff):

Have you been convicted of any other criminal offense?
_____ Yes   _____ No
If yes, please explain:

Are there any moving violations on your driving record?
_____ Yes   _____ No
If yes, please explain:

To the best of your knowledge, is there anything from your past that would disqualify you from working with children and youth?
_____ Yes   _____ No
If yes, please explain:

Personal References

1) Name:_____

   Address: _____

   City_____ State_____ Zip _____

   Phone:(____)_____ Relationship: _____

2) Name:_____

   Address: _____

   City_____ State_____ Zip _____

   Phone:(____)_____ Relationship: _____

3) Name:_____

    Address: _____

    City_____ State____ Zip _____

    Phone:(___)_____ Relationship: _____

On a separate piece of paper, please provide a brief testimony of your Christian faith journey.

Applicant's Statement

The information I have given in this application is correct and complete to the best of my knowledge. I agree that false information or significant omissions may disqualify me from further consideration for service and may be considered justification for dismissal if discovered at a later date. I also authorize First Church to contact references and to conduct background checks that could include review of personal records such as driving, police, etc.

Should my application be accepted, I agree to be bound by the constitution and policies of First Church.

_____Date:_____
Applicant's Signature

_____Date:_____
Staff Signature

APPENDIX C
INTEREST AND SKILL SURVEY

"There are different kinds of gifts, but the same Spirit. There are different kinds of service, but the same Lord. There are different kinds of working, but the same God works all of them in all men."

I Corinthians 12:4-6

This survey is designed to give you an opportunity to use your gifts and talents to serve the body. Completing this survey does not obligate you to a job.

Name_____ Phone _____
Home Address _____
City_____State_____Zip _____
Profession/Occupation _____

Place an X in the appropriate columns:

AREA OF MINISTRY		HAVE SERVED	WILLING
EDUCATION/DISCIPLESHIP			
Lead small-group Bible study:	Junior High		
	Senior High		
Teach a Sunday school class:	Junior High		
	Senior High		
Teach a class (doctrine, confirmation)			
Teach an elective/short-term class	Topic_____		
Be a guest speaker on a topic	Topic_____		
ACTIVITIES			
Coach a sports team	Sport_____		
Attend special youth group events			
Play a musical instrument	Instrument_____		
Lead group singing			
Host youth group events			
Share specialty area (puppet ministry, drama etc.)	Area_____		
Work on service projects			
Help with a mission trip			

AREA OF MINISTRY	HAVE SERVED	WILLING
RELATIONAL		
Be involved in personal mentoring		
Be involved in outreach to unchurched teens		
Attend school activities		
Lead a personal support group for teens		
Be involved in nurture and counseling		
SUPPORT		
Permission to use cabin, boat, etc.		
Work on publicity/promotion		
Drive to events		
Drive the bus		
Work on audio visual		
Provide refreshments		
Kitchen help		
Office support		
Phone calling		
Assist in fundraising events		
Do computer work		
Prepare mailings/newsletters		

ENDNOTES

Introduction

[1] Roehlkepartain, Jolene L., *Youth Ministry: Its Impact on Church Growth* (Loveland, Co.: Thom Schultz Publishing, Inc.)

[2] Jim Burns, *Youth Builder* (Eugene, OR: Harvest House, 1988), 131

Chapter One: How to Build an Effective Volunteer Team

[1] Bertolini, Dewey, *Back to the Heart of Youth Work* (Wheaton, Ill.: Victor, 1989)

[2] McKinnon, Greg, "Why Youth Workers Sabotoge Volunteers," *Youthworker Journal* (Winter 1986): 22-23.

NOTES

NOTES

NOTES

The needs of youth are changing. How will you keep up?

Effective youth ministry takes more than good intentions. It takes theological reflection, an understanding of adolescents, and the skills necessary to reach them.

We at Youth Leadership understand the value of relational ministry. Our purpose is to train adults to share the Gospel of Jesus Christ dynamically with young people and their families through relational, incarnational ministry.

Graduate Degree Program

Youth Leadership's graduate degree program in youth ministry is the oldest in the country. In cooperation with Bethel and Luther Seminaries in St. Paul, Minnesota the program offers an M.A. in Youth Ministry and an M.Div. with a youth ministry concentration.

Summer Institute

An intensive week of youth ministry training, the Institute may be attended for your continuing education or for graduate credit.

Professional & Volunteer Training

Youth Leadership also provides quarterly seminars for volunteer youth workers and monthly seminars for professionals in the field.

Consulting & Speaking

Youth Leadership staff members speak to thousands of youth workers, parents, and teenagers each year around the country. They also provide on-site training upon request.

Dennis "Tiger" McLuen is the Director of Youth Leadership and instructor of youth ministry at both Bethel and Luther Seminaries.

Equipping Adults to Serve Effectively Since 1967

YOUTH LEADERSHIP • CENTER FOR YOUTH & FAMILY MINISTRY

122 West Franklin Avenue • Suite 510 • Minneapolis, MN 55404 • 612/870-3632